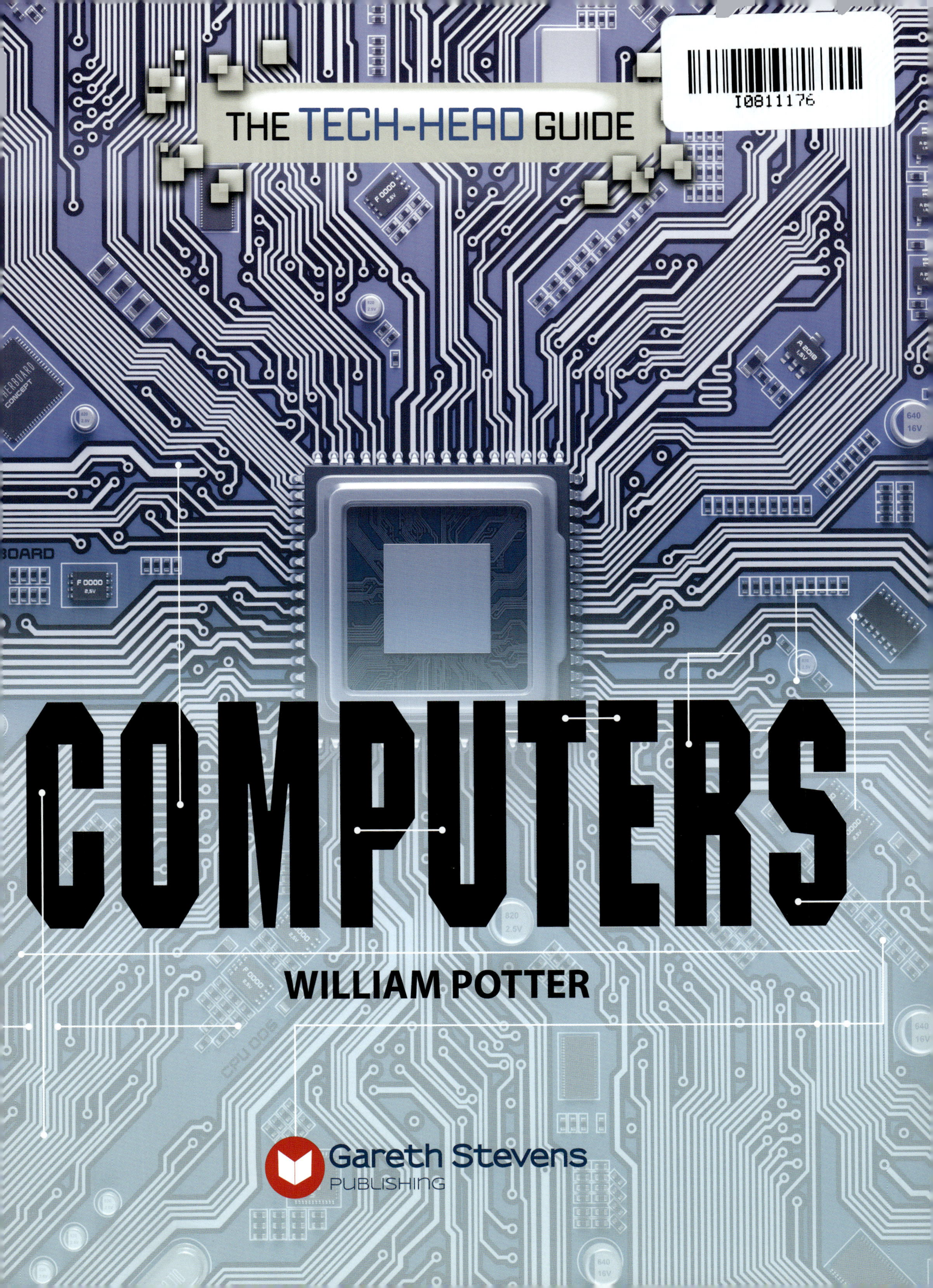

THE TECH-HEAD GUIDE

COMPUTERS

WILLIAM POTTER

Gareth Stevens PUBLISHING

Please visit our website, www.garethstevens.com. For a free color catalog of all our high-quality books, call toll free 1-800-542-2595 or fax 1-877-542-2596.

Cataloging-in-Publication Data

Names: Potter, William.
Title: Computers / William Potter.
Description: New York : Gareth Stevens Publishing, 2023. | Series: The tech-head guide | Includes glossary and index.
Identifiers: ISBN 9781538277416 (pbk.) | ISBN 9781538277430 (library bound) | ISBN 9781538277423 (6pack) | ISBN 9781538277447 (ebook)
Subjects: LCSH: Computers--Juvenile literature. | Computer systems--Juvenile literature.
Classification: LCC QA76.23 P688 2023 | DDC 004--dc23

Published in 2023 by
Gareth Stevens Publishing
29 E. 21st Street
New York, NY 10010

Editor: Elise Short
Design concept: Wild Pixel Ltd
Designer: Jason Billin

Picture Credits
Alamy: Agencja Fotografinza Caro 29br; Ian Dagnall 25b; GL Archive 12bl; Iamapress back cover br, 29bl; Andrew Kitching 13t; Moviestore Collection/© Disney 19b; Mark Richardson 27t. Dreamstime: Sabljak 9br. Epic Games 25c.Getty Images: 10bl; Agustinc back cover bl, 20cr; Dave M Bennet 27br; Dan Callister 14cr; Fotosearch 8cl; Bill Hinton 17br; Kim Kulish 14-15bg, 15b; Mark Madeo/Future Pub: 8cr Tom Mihalek/AFP: 24br; Science & Society PL: back cover t, 6-7bg, 6b, 7t, 7c, 9cl. NASA: PD 7b. NASC: 14cl. PRNewsFoto-Ducere Technologies :27cl. Science Photo Library: CERN 16cl. Sega: 25tr. Shutterstock: ACIcon 4bcl; Adragan 15tl; agsandrew front cover bgc; Aleksangel 4bl, 5bcl; america365 front cover cl; andik76 24-25bg; Astira 5bcl; Atstock Productions 22c; AVIcon 4bcr; 16cr; Radhu Bercan 16cr; Berkah Icon 5blc, 5bccl; Christian Bertrand 26br; bestfoto77 8-9 bg; Canadapanda 9tr; CAPToro 5bc; Cornel Constantin 11cr; Graeme Dawes 12cr; defmorph 5blcc; Dr Manager 4-5bg; Elena11 10-11bg; elenabsi 23br; Evdokimov Maxim 18-19bg; Nico ElNino 17bl; Fireofheart 20b; Nor Gal 10br; Gorodenkoff 19t; Grenar 4br; Andrew Heffernan 4blcc; Anna Hoychuk 26c; IB Photography 9cl; IMG 191 9bl; irbis pictures 18cl; ittoilmatar front cover tl; Alesia Kan 13cl; Jane Kelly 23tl; kpatyhka 23tr; ksenvitain 4brcc; Leremy 22b; Illia Levchenko front cover main; Lightspring 20cl; Lineicons freebird front cover drop-ins, 4bc; Oleksiy Mark17tr; Maxx-Studio 1; metamorworks 28-29bg; Oleksandr Molotkovych 5br; Moviestore/Rex 19c; Agus Mul 5bcr; Nicescene 21tl; NinjaStudio 4brc; Oakview Studios 5brcc; omihay 13cr; padu_foto 25tl; paulista 11bra; 26bl Peppinnuzzo 26bl; Sergey Peterman 5c; Phonlamai Photo 11crb; pking4th front cover drop-ins; Poznauakov front cover cr; PrinceofLove 18br; ra studio 28br; Rawpixel.com 10-11c; Maziar Roohl front cover tr; Rost9 29tr; sdecoret front cover bg, 23bl; Anton Shaparenko 4blc, 4bccl; Sviatlana Sheina 5bl; solarseven 20-21bg spainter vfx 2-3bg, 12-13bg, 26-27bg; Cristian Storto 8bl; Tzido Sun 22-23bg; SWevil 21tr; Navin Tar 5tr; Tinxi 24bl; wavebreakmedia 16-17bg, 30-31bg, 32bg; weera. otp 10cl; Who is Danny 17tl. Wikimedia Commons: Michael Holley/PD 8br; Carlos Jones/ORNL CC 2 15c; Kenneth Lu/CC 2 24c; Marsyas /CC 2.5 6c.

Printed in the United States of America

CPSIA compliance information: Batch #CSGS23: For further information contact Gareth Stevens, New York, New York at 1-800-542-2595.

CONTENTS

COMPUTER WORLD

Computers are all around us. From the smartphones in our pockets to weather-mapping supercomputers, we're now connected through these clever machines. They play an increasing role in our lives.

ANCIENT AND MODERN

In this book, you'll find out about ancient calculating machines, code-cracking computers, the first room-filling supercomputers, video games, amazing apps, and the mind-boggling future of quantum computing, augmented reality, and artificial intelligence. Plus, you'll pick up all the techie words you need to know to be computer-savvy.

TIMELINE

- **1801** Joseph Marie Jacquard invents a loom that uses punchcard commands
- **1844** Ava Lovelace writes the first computer program (page 12)
- **1939** Code-cracking British **Bombe** designed at Bletchley Park, UK (page 7)
- **1947** Invention of transistor by William Shockley, John Bardeen, and Walter Brattai (page 8)
- **1949** First practical stored-program computer, **EDSAC**
- **1956** First keyboard input to computer
- **1958** U.S. electrical engineer Jack Kilby creates first integrated circuit
- **1964** **BASIC** programming language introduced (page 13)
- **1968** **Apollo Guidance Computer** debuts (page 14)
- **1972** Computer game ***Pong*** released (page 24)

WHAT IS A COMPUTER?

Computers are machines that can be programmed to solve problems using mathematics or logic. They were developed from simple calculators, such as the **abacus**, and mechanical devices, such as the **difference engine** (see page 6). The introduction of electronics, **transistors**, and **microchips** has led to smaller and faster computers that are used for far more than calculations.

CHIPS WITH EVERYTHING

You might not realize how much computers help you day to day, not just through desktop PCs and smartphones. Computer chips help program microwave ovens, many fridges, and toasters; set the heating for our homes; control street and traffic lights; help us pay with debit cards; and drive cars, trains, and planes.

This book was written on a computer word processor. Computers were used to check facts online, source photos, design the layout, and deliver the files to a printer. Books can be ordered online, with a computer-controlled robot collecting the book for delivery, or downloaded and read on a computer screen. Turn the page to log in!

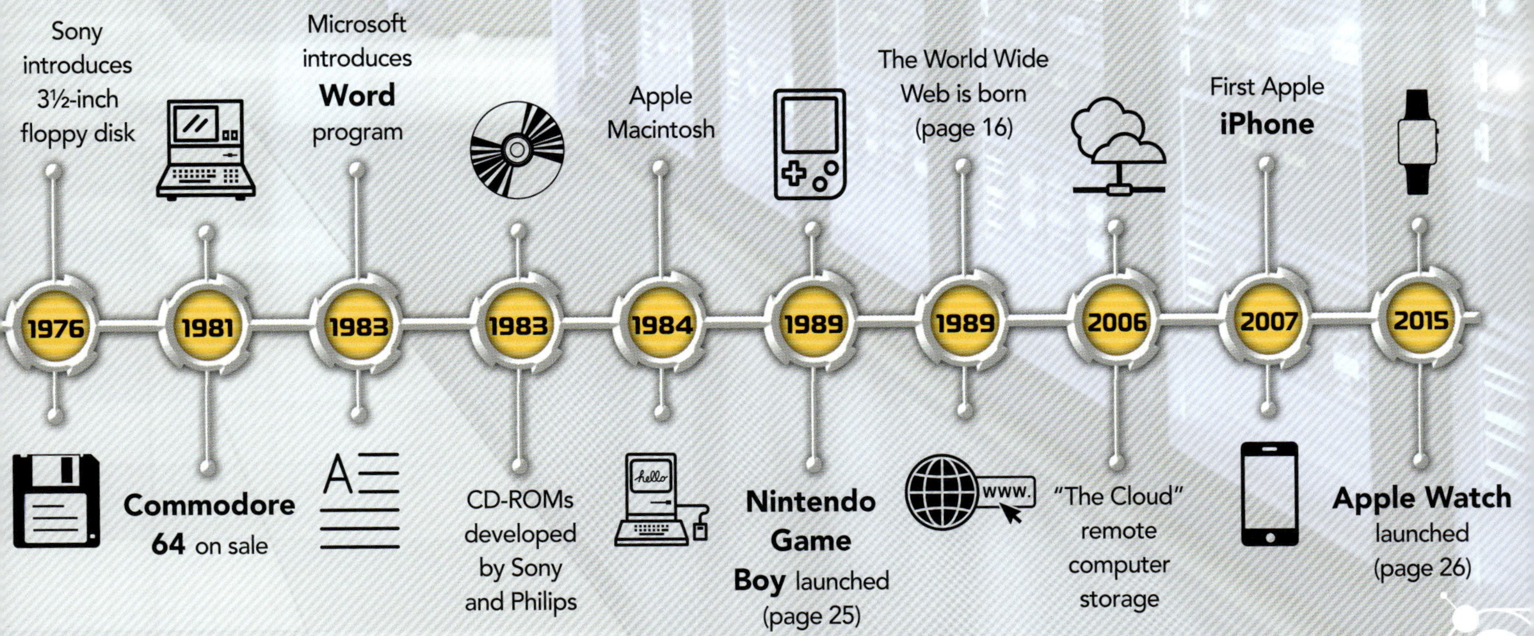

HISTORY OF THE COMPUTER

Before the use of electricity, humans built machines to do complicated calculations. These early geared machines were engineering marvels and the forerunners of today's computers.

DEEP HISTORY

In 1902, divers off the coast of Greece discovered a rusting device (right) in a shipwreck dating from around 100 BCE. Scientists worked out that this ancient **Antikythera mechanism** used gears that could map the position of the moon and planets. It is often described as the world's first computer.

MAKING A DIFFERENCE

In the early 19th century, the British mathematician and engineer **Charles Babbage** designed a machine that could automatically solve complex equations. Called the **difference engine**, it worked through a system of toothed gears. The device (below) was not built until 1991, long after Babbage died, but it worked like a dream!

SECRET PLANS

World War II (1939–45) saw a surge in computer design. The German inventor **Konrad Zuse** built the **Z3**, the first automatic electronic computer controlled by **programs** (see page 12), but it was destroyed in a bombing raid. At the UK's top-secret Bletchley Park, **Alan Turing** led a team working on code-breaking machines, the **Bombe** (above) and **Colossus**. In the USA, engineers spent two years constructing **ENIAC**, a massive, missile-tracking computer a thousand times faster than previous machines.

MULTI-PURPOSE

The first computer to be easily reprogrammed for different tasks was called **EDSAC** (Electronic Delay Storage Automatic Calculator). Completed at Cambridge University in 1949, EDSAC (below) received instructions to work out mathematical problems on punched paper tape and used 3,500 valves and tubes of mercury to pass on information. Results were printed on paper.

HUMAN COMPUTERS

The word "computer" was first used to describe people whose job it was to do difficult mathematical work. One team of female computers, led by **Katherine Johnson** (right), helped calculate flight paths for NASA's early space program. The word "computer" started to mean the machine by 1945.

LET'S GET PERSONAL

The first electronic computers were huge and expensive beasts, designed for scientists, the armed services, and big business. For computers to be accepted into the home they needed to be smaller ... and a lot cheaper!

PERSONAL SUCCESS

The first **personal computer** (PC) is considered to be the **Altair 8800**. This computer kit sold for about $300 in 1975. It made computing affordable for home enthusiasts and inspired people such as **Bill Gates** (see page 14) and **Paul Allen** to get into computing. They launched the **software** company **Microsoft** together.

CHIP REVOLUTION

Early computers used fragile vacuum tubes (see above), or valves, to send instructions by switching electrical currents on and off. A huge leap forward came in 1957 with the invention of the **transistor**. These could do the same job but were much smaller and used less power. The integrated circuit, or computer chip, with several tiny transistors linked together, followed in 1958.

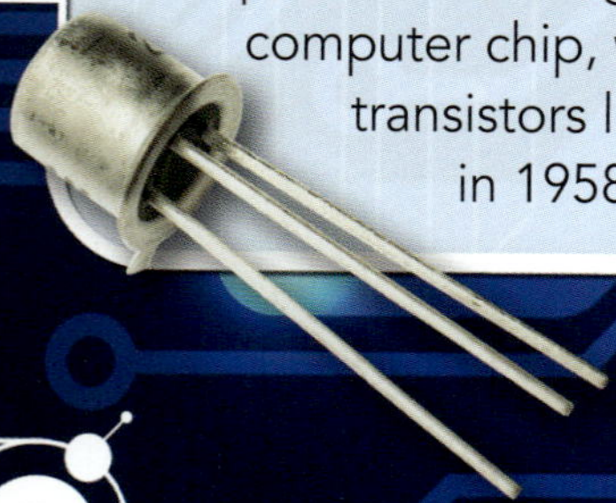

APPLE BITES

In 1976, **Steve Jobs** and **Steve Wozniak** showed off their simple circuit board (see page 11), which they called **Apple-1**. They followed it up a year later with a complete computer using color graphics. This **Apple II** (below) sold in millions. These were the first products from a company that would go on to dominate computer tech.

SMALLER AND MORE POWERFUL

Tech companies have managed to squeeze more and tinier transistors on to computer chips. Now the workings of a high-powered desktop computer can be hidden behind a slim screen, while cables have been replaced by wire-free **Wi-Fi** and **Bluetooth** connections.

OLD-SCHOOL TECH

Many home computers in the 1970s and '80s often did not have their own screens. They had to be plugged into a TV. Most, like the **Atari 400**, the **Sinclair ZX-Spectrum**, and the best-selling home computer of all-time, the **Commodore 64** (below right), were good for playing video games, aided by the introduction of the **joystick** control (below left). At first, programs were uploaded using a cassette-tape player or **floppy disks** (above).

PORTABLE POWER

Where once computers filled rooms, now superfast laptops or tablets can be carried in a backpack. The processing power of a typical modern smartphone is more powerful than all the computers used by NASA to send astronauts to the moon in 1969.

INSIDE THE BOX

While parts get smaller, faster, and more efficient, the basic components of a desktop computer are much the same. Here's a look at what makes your computer tick.

INPUT

A **mouse**, **keyboard**, or **trackpad** gives instructions to the computer.

CENTRAL CONTROL

The **CPU** (central processing unit) or **microprocessor** is the brain of the computer. It receives commands from the mouse or keyboard and controls operations. The CPU is a ceramic slab with a silicon chip inside. The speed of the CPU is a measure of how many instructions it can deal with in a second, rated in gigahertz (GHz).

WOOD WORK

The first computer **mouse** was carved from wood. Made by **Douglas Englebart** in 1964 to move a cursor (arrow) around a computer screen, it was named a "mouse" because the connecting cord looked like a tail.

COMPUTER CHIPS

The silicon chip in the CPU is made up of electronic **integrated circuits** with billions of microscopic components, including **transistors**.

MEMORY MATTERS

Computers have a short-term memory, **RAM** (random-access memory), used for temporary tasks, and a long-term memory on a **hard drive** that stores files and programs even when the computer is switched off.

SCREEN TIME

You need a monitor screen to see what you are typing and where to click. The screen image is made up of tiny dots called **pixels** that change color on command.

ZEROS AND ONES

Information, or **data** (numbers, letters, images, and sounds), is stored and shared in a computer in the form of **binary code**–a series of zeros and ones. The **transistors** in a computer chip act like gates, stopping the flow of electrical current or allowing it to pass. No current = 0. A flow of current = 1. A zero or one is called a **bit**. Eight bits equal a **byte** (b). A million bytes = 1 megabyte (Mb). Each chip can hold billions of transistors, each just 14 **nanometers** (nm) long – about 5,000 times thinner than a human hair!

Human hair
About 75,000 nm wide

Red blood cell
About 6,000 nm wide

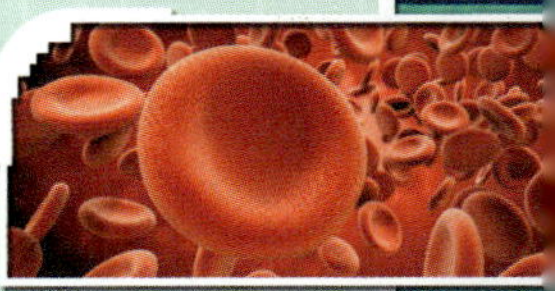

Bacterium
About 1,000 nm wide

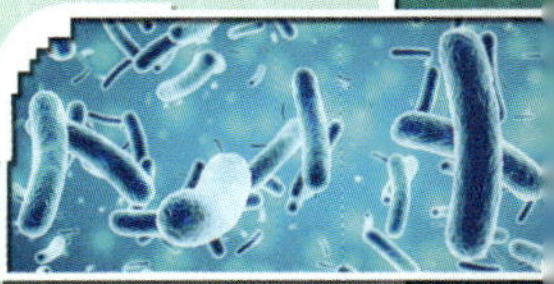

Transistor
14 nm wide

ALL TOGETHER NOW

The CPU and memory sit on a flat, printed circuit board called the **motherboard**. This connects all the parts in a computer, letting the CPU receive commands and send instructions to other parts, such as the hard drive or DVD player.

SOFTWARE SECRETS

Inside your computer hardware, different kinds of programs (software) can be running games, web browsers, videos, or design programs. You can choose what to install on your computer and even learn to program with a little coding knowledge.

PROGRAM NUMBER ONE

In the early 19th century, **Charles Babbage** (see page 6) worked on his designs for an **analytical engine**, which used an elaborate punchcard operating system. His colleague, the mathematician **Ada Lovelace**, saw the potential for Babbage's machine to solve complex calculations. She worked out an example which is considered the first computer program.

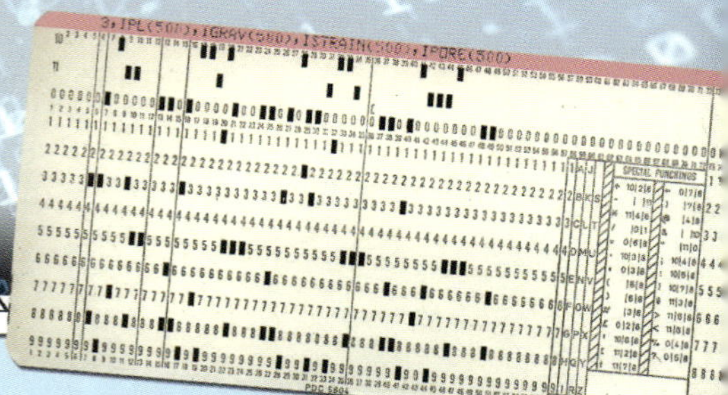

PUNCHCARD

The first computers received **binary code** instructions from punched paper cards or tape. Each hole equalled 1 and no hole equalled 0.

ON THE MENU

Computer programs work using **algorithms**. These are a series of steps for the program to follow to find the right answer. Like a recipe, the steps have to be followed in the right order to get the correct result.

BACK TO BASICS

Programmers now type in coded instructions for a computer using computer languages. **BASIC** (eginner's All-purpose Symbolic Instruction Code) was a computer language designed in 1964 for students and home-computer users. It used strings of commands with Y (Yes) and N (No) options, and was in use until the late 1980s, when more visual languages were introduced.

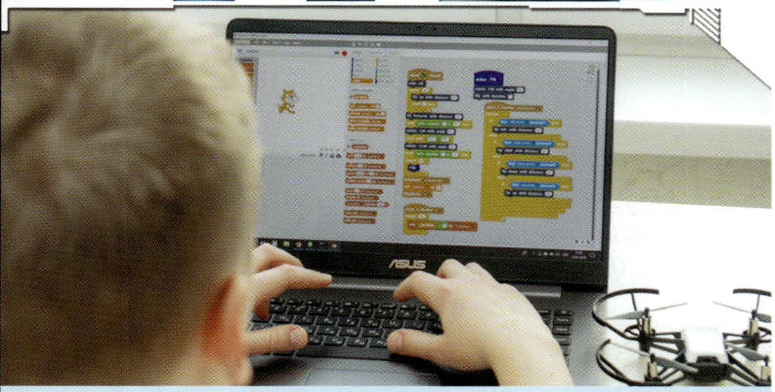

MANY VOICES

Different computer languages have been designed for specific purposes. For example:

FORTRAN (Formula Translation) Suited for mathematical calculations

COBOL (Common Business-Orientated Language) For business software

LISP Used by scientists involved in artificial intelligence (AI)

JAVA This popular language is used to build apps for Android phones

SCRATCH Simple visual language used to teach kids how to program

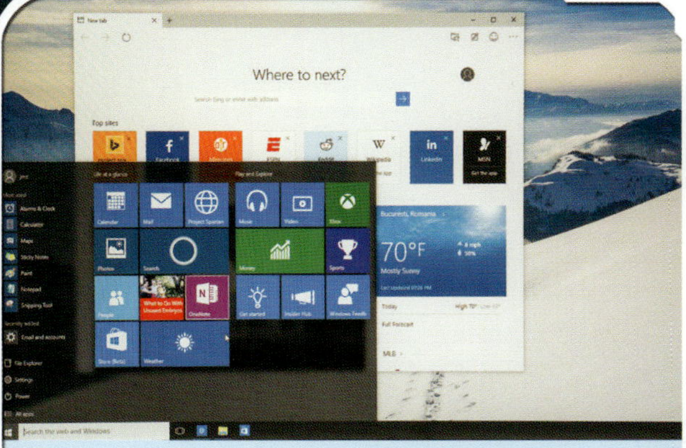

PICTURE PERFECT

While programmers deal with long lines of code, general home-computer users need something simpler to work with. That's where an **operating system** (OS) comes in. This graphical interface puts words and pictures on screen for the user to click and drag to complete tasks. Popular operating systems include **Windows**, **macOS**, and **Linux**.

DIGITAL DATA

Computer technology has moved from room-filling, punchcard-operated machines to pocket-sized powerhouses at incredible speed. Here are some astounding facts about computers old and new.

MOON SHOT

Fifty years ago, NASA sent men to the moon with a computer less powerful than the microprocessor used in a modern-day microwave oven. And yet, with just 64 KB of memory and a tiny speed of 0.043 MHz, the **Apollo Guidance Computer** (AGC) helped steer the crew of **Apollo 11** from Earth to the moon and back.

HEAVY WEIGHT

Five megabyte or MB of computer memory is nothing nowadays (about the same file size as a song), with plug-in storage sticks able to carry several gigabytes or GB (1 GB = 1,000 MB). In 1956 you needed a forklift to move this kind of memory! The **IBM 305 RAMAC** computer was one of the first computers with a 5 MB hard disk drive but it weighed over a ton!

HI-TECH HOME

Computer software company **Microsoft** made CEO **Bill Gates** one of the richest people on the planet. He used some of his money to build his $127 million mansion, Xanadu 2.0. The computer-designed home took seven years to construct and includes $80,000 worth of computer screens in the walls, displaying a choice of paintings or photographs. Visitors are given an electronic pin which changes room lighting, music, and temperature to match their preferences.

COMPUTER CASH

With internet shopping, credit-card use, and electronic payments, cash is being used less. Current estimates are that 90 percent of money is held in computers, compared to 10 percent in notes and coins. There is even money called **cryptocurrency** that doesn't exist in physical form and is used online without a central bank.

RACE LEADER

The world's fastest supercomputer is currently the **IBM Summit** at Oak Ridge National Laboratory, Tennessee. The machine covers the space of two basketball courts, with 136 miles (219 km) of cabling, 250 petabytes (250,000 million million bytes) of storage and 9,216 IBM POWER9 CPUs. It can reach computing speeds of 200 petaflops (that's 200,000 million million operations a second)!

HIGHER TECH

Supercomputers are the biggest and fastest of computer tech, able to do the most complex calculations. Among the tasks supercomputers are working on are predicting earthquakes, forecasting world weather, simulating the human brain, and even trying to recreate the process of the big bang that began the universe.

CONNECTED

Over half the world's population is connected online. The internet has given computer users the ability to search for and share information and entertainment.

WORLD WIDE WEB

The internet was invented in 1969 as a way for researchers to share data with other computer users. The **APRANET** (Advanced Research Projects Agency Network) connected four U.S. universities via phone lines, but users had to search inside folders and files to find what they needed.

In 1989, at the European research organization **CERN**, British engineer **Tim Berners-Lee** (above) designed a more intuitive **World Wide Web** that allowed users to click on text **hyperlinks** to jump to files on separate web pages. This was the first **web browser**. You can still visit the first website at *info.cern.ch*.

Programs designed to find content in any public website followed. These **search engines** now provide results from millions and millions of websites in seconds.

THE LONG WAIT

In 1993, the average home internet user had to use a phone to dial and make a connection. Speeds were restricted to 56 kbps (kilobytes per second). Today the global average for internet speed is 11 megabytes per second (mbps) and the fastest recorded average speed is 67.5 mpbs. That's more than a thousand times faster than in 1993.

SPEEDING UP

With today's high-speed **broadband**, users can make video calls and stream HD-quality films. Speeds are predicted to reach 1 terabit per second soon (1,000 times faster than 1 GB per second) – enough to download a whole HD TV box set in a second)!

CHATTERBOX

The first **email** (short for electronic mail) was sent in 1971 by computer engineer Ray Tomlinson. Emails allow you to send messages and attachments such as photos and documents. While more than 203 billion emails are sent around the world every day, they are being partly replaced by more informal communication, such as **messaging apps** and the use of **emojis**.

IN THE CLOUD

Cloud computing lets computer users save files on another computer hard drive over the internet by renting space from a company **data center**. A user can access and update their files securely online just as they would on their home computer.

SOCIAL SCENE

The internet has allowed creative (and chatty!) people to reach a new audience, sharing their opinions, music, or videos. **Bloggers** and **vloggers** (video bloggers) can become famous with millions of online followers. Social media has become the meeting place for many people and allows friends in distant countries to stay in regular contact.

THE DARK SIDE

Only a small part of the internet can be seen by the casual browser. The largest part of the internet is a **deep web** that cannot be found using a **search engine**. The deep web holds private data that can only be found if you know the web address. Even more hidden is the so-called **dark web**, which can only be reached using special software. As users cannot be tracked, this is a place where secret and criminal activity takes place.

CREATIVE CODE

Computers are not just for juggling numbers and writing essays. They are the new paintbrushes, musical instruments, and film cameras, helping artists create amazing images, music, and films.

FUTURE FANTASY

Computer software can be used with a mouse or a **stylus** on a **trackpad** to create comic-book illustrations or fantasy paintings. Special effects can be added to images to produce photo-realistic paintings or collages. The computer can even be set to run free and design its own machine art, such as repeated fractal patterns or art made using **algorithms**.

ALTERED STATES

With software able to duplicate hair, skin, and fabrics, it is easy for editors to **airbrush** photographs and produce a "perfect" image, hiding a model's wrinkles or blemishes so well that the viewer may never know it's fake.

IN THE MIX

Most recording studios now record digitally rather than using magnetic tape. This allows studio engineers to use software to cut, swap, and repair the parts played by musicians and to add echo and other sound effects to produce the final mix. Computer trickery can also fix off-pitch vocals by using the program **Auto-Tune**.

HOME STUDIO

Cheaper computer technology has meant budding musicians can create music at home. Digital instruments can be plugged in or samples imported. And, with music files downloaded or streamed over the internet, computers have made it possible for musicians to deliver tunes directly to fans.

COMPUTER CINEMA

The first entirely 3D computer-generated sequence in a film appeared in 1982's ***Star Trek II: The Wrath of Khan***. In the same year, the virtual-reality adventure ***Tron*** (right) included 15 minutes of fully computer-generated footage. Now animators are using programs to add **CGI (computer-generated imagery)** to many blockbusters for superhero powers, special effects, and motion capture and even to make actors appear younger!

PIXEL POWER

Pixar Studios' 1995 hit *Toy Story* led the way for feature-length digitally animated films. Creating a 90-minute computer-animated film requires a huge team of illustrators and animators and massive amounts of computer power. It can take more than 24 hours to **render**, or process, each frame of animation–and there are 24 of them for every second of film! The studio has a "**render farm**" that is the equivalent of a supercomputer of 2,000 machines to complete the job!

UNDER ATTACK

Watch out! Malware (malicious software) is programs designed to cause problems on your computer. They can be disguised as an attachment in an email and, once opened, deny you access to your files or steal your private information.

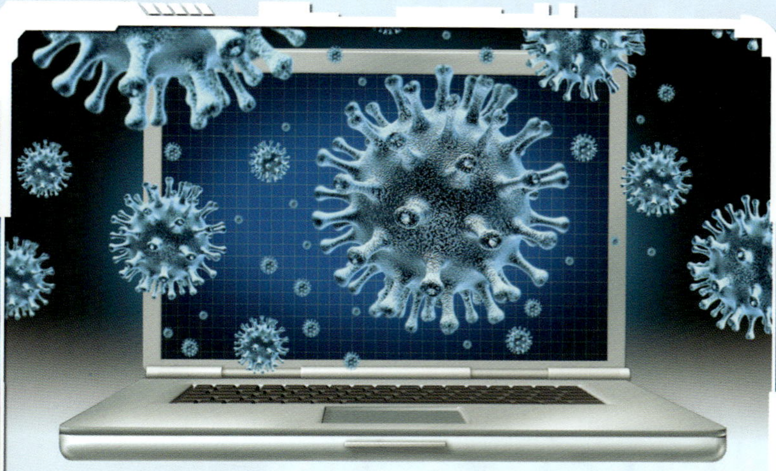

GETTING INSIDE

Viruses are sneaky patches of code that can slow down your computer's functions and corrupt files so you can no longer open them. **Worms** are similar, but this software can copy itself and spread further. **Trojans**, like the legendary Trojan horse, are viruses disguised as trusted software.

WATCHING YOU

Spyware is a type of program that records what you do on your computer. It can recognise the keys you press to type in passwords, then use them to get into your private data.

ZOMBIE ALERT!

Some malware is designed to let others gain access to your computer, grab your secret passwords, and use your machine as a **zombie computer** to send out even more malware. It can steal contact details and send your friends **spam** or junk email from your address.

THE PAY-OFF

Ransomware is a program that adds **encryption code** to files on your computer so you can't open them. The hacker who sends it to your computer may then demand a payment to provide a password for you to unlock the files.

CYBER-STRIKE

Sometimes the computers of whole companies and organizations are targeted in a **cyberattack** to disrupt, disable, or steal information. Teams of **hackers**–experts at illegally breaking into computer systems–work to find security weaknesses and then add their own code or controls.

IT'S A STEAL!

Scammers gather email addresses and send out emails that, for example, claim you are owed money or have won a prize. To claim it, they say you need to share your bank details or send a donation. Of course, it's all a trick to grab cash!

DON'T PANIC!

Turn the page for some top tips on how to dodge the dangers!

STAY SAFE

How can you avoid the worst of the internet, keep your secrets, and keep your computer running safely? There are a few good rules and practices worth remembering.

WHO TO TRUST

Follow these simple rules to stay safe online:

- Beware of strangers. The person you're talking to online could be pretending to be someone else.
- Think twice about sharing images of yourself, because once they are online, anyone can get ahold of them.
- Don't share any personal information, such as your address, email, or phone number.
- Alert your parents if a stranger asks to meet you.

BEAT THE BULLIES

Some people think it's fun to be cruel to others online, posting nasty comments and pictures. Often you won't know who's behind it. Don't encourage them by replying to their taunts. The best way to deal with these **cyberbullies** is to **block** them and report their behavior to the social-media website they used.

DON'T GET ATTACHED

Most viruses find their way on to your computer as an email attachment. If you don't trust the source or think there's something wrong about an email you've received, delete it and never open any attached files.

LOGGING IN

To register with some websites you'll need a password. Don't choose anything anyone could work out. And keep it secret! Many websites sensibly ask for a password that includes capital and lowercase letters, numbers, and symbols, which is hard to guess. Don't forget to use different passwords for each website and account to help keep your accounts safe. And, once you've finished on a website, always log out again!

SECURITY SERVICE

There are many brands of security software you can install on your computer. The companies that build the software are constantly updating their programs to defend against new malware, so keep your security software updated too.

NETIQUETTE

And, finally, do your bit to keep the internet a happy place. Be polite online. Even if something annoys you, you don't have to let off steam and be rude to a stranger online.

GAME ON

The video-game industry is worth billions worldwide, with players demanding ever-faster hardware and more impressive graphics and sound from their computers.

FIRST HIT

In the 1950s, computers were too precious and expensive to be used for playing games. Then, in 1962, one machine, the **DEC PDP-1** got into the hands of students at the Massachusetts Institute of Technology (MIT in Boston), who tested it with a program called ***Spacewar!*** This simple duelling game between two starships (right) became a hit with programming students, making it the first widely available computer game.

HOME ARCADE

Coin-operated arcade games were a hit in the 1970s and gradually made their way to game consoles for the home. Early adaptations were hits such as ***Space Invaders*** and ***Pac-Man***. One simple game that took off on home computers was ***Pong***. This basic table-tennis game with vertically sliding bats (above) was released for game consoles by Atari in 1975.

THE NEW CHAMP

Chess was an early game to be adapted for computers and a test for computer sophistication. In 1977, a milestone was hit when the IBM computer **Deep Blue** defeated the world chess champion Garry Kasparov (above left).

BRICK BY BRICK

The best-selling game ***Tetris*** launched on the Nintendo hand-held **Game Boy** in 1989. Programmed by Russian designer Alexey Pajitnov, the simple but addictive game involves descending bricks that need to be arranged into a wall. The Game Boy was not the first handheld gaming device, but it was easily the most popular, selling over 118 million of its early models.

NEW DIMENSION

In the 1990s, increased processor power allowed 3D computer graphics to be used in games. ***Virtua Racing*** (1992) and ***Super Mario 64*** (1996) were early hits on home consoles such as the Sony PlayStation and Nintendo 64.

TEAM PLAYERS

Fast internet connections have allowed communities to join online role-playing games such as ***World of Warcraft*** (2004), the massively popular environment-building ***Minecraft***, and ***Fortnite*** (left), a shoot-'em-up game where players join forces. This advance in technology has also led to a rise in the popularity and coverage of **esports** (electronic sports) in a wide range of games played by professional players.

MOBILE MADNESS

The computer power of a modern smartphone has delivered a huge market for gaming apps. The addictive smartphone game ***Angry Birds*** became a huge hit, with over 3 billion free downloads following its 2009 debut. Fast mobile data (mobile internet access) and GPS has made outdoor **augmented reality (AR)** games a reality, with computer-generated layers added over a camera's view. 2016's ***Pokémon Go*** had 500 million downloads in its first year, with players seeking animated characters in a real-world environment.

CYBER COOL

You don't have to be stuck at a desk to get connected. Thanks to tiny microprocessors, Wi-Fi, and GPS, you can be accessing and sharing computer data when you're out and about with wearable tech.

TWIST THE WRIST

Smartwatches act like mini smartphones, receiving calls and alerts from email or social media, reminding you of appointments, checking the weather, playing music ... and they tell the time too! **Activity trackers** have fewer apps but also use **GPS** information to keep tabs on how far and how fast you move. They can even act as a heart-rate monitor for a more detailed health record.

EYE SPY

The tech did not take off as much as expected, but **smartglasses** may still have their day. Invented in the 2010s, smartglasses worn as a pair of spectacles display info such as the weather forecast, phone calls, and photos. The smartglasses are controlled by voice command and a small touchpad on the side and can access maps, local information, and translations.

VIRTUALLY THERE

For an even more immersive experience, **virtual reality (VR)** headsets can put you in an entirely computer-generated environment. The headsets track your head movement and display 3D imagery that you can move around in and investigate. With a **VR glove**, you can even manipulate objects in this virtual 3D world.

REMOTE CONTROL

Thanks to GPS tracking, convicted criminals can be restricted to their home or neighborhood rather than put in jail. **Electronic tags** are secure devices worn on the ankle that can be hidden under pants. They record the movements of the wearer to make sure they do not stray beyond an agreed area. Any rule-breaking or tampering with the tag is reported to the police.

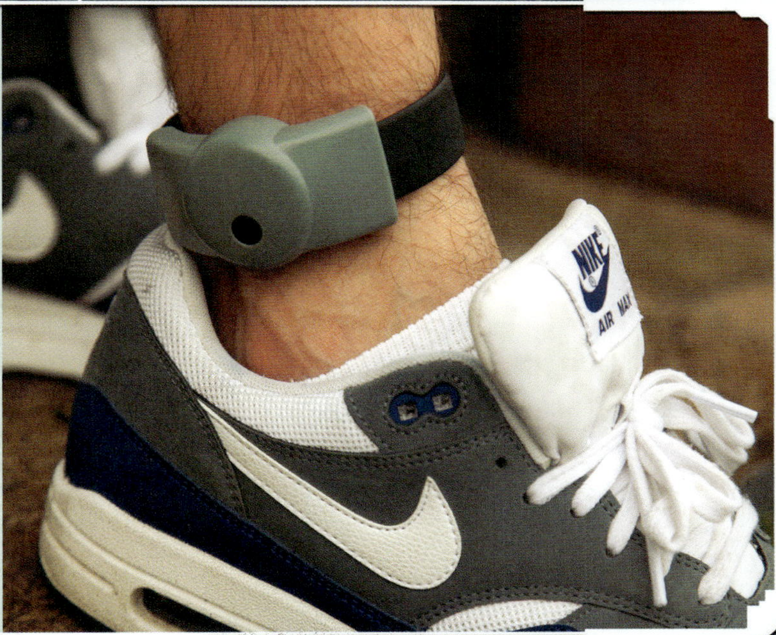

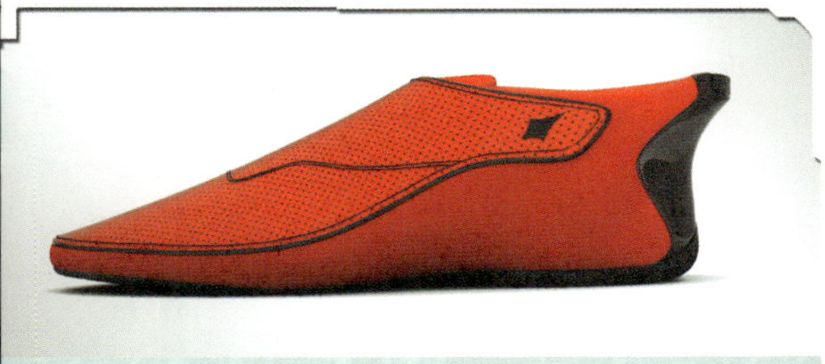

SHOE SENSORS

Imagine if your shoes could lead you where you want to go. Well, that's what these Bluetooth-enabled **smartshoes** are designed to do by linking up with a mapping app on a smartphone. First you choose your destination, then the shoes connect with the phone and each shoe buzzes to tell you to turn left or right and announce when you've arrived! They could provide assistance for millions of visually impaired walkers.

DRESSED FOR DATA

How about the full wardrobe? In 2012, singer Nicole Scherzinger demonstrated a stylish, hi-tech dress designed by Cute Circuit which shares tweets lit up by 2,000 LED lights on the fabric!

THE NEXT LEVEL

What's next for computer technology? Can microchips get any more micro? Will we give up on keyboards and talk or wave to our machines? Here are some ideas about the future of computer tech.

THE INTERNET OF THINGS

The internet is not just for people. Hi-tech gadgets in the home can automatically share information via **Wi-Fi**. Artificial intelligence in a fridge can recognize that you are out of milk and order a delivery, while a smart thermostat lets you regulate the temperature in your home remotely and learns your habits. This ability of devices to work online is called the **Internet of Things**.

LENS FLAIR

The technology used in smartglasses (see page 26) has already been shrunk down to work in contact lenses using **holographic optics** tech. In the future you will be able to access info with a blink and see names, directions, and encyclopedia info displayed as a hologram in front of you, as **AR (augmented reality)** apps do today.

WAVE MOTION

Computers, smartphones and **smartspeakers** can already understand voice commands. How will we communicate with tech in the future? Gesture recognition used in **Microsoft Kinect** and the **Nintendo Wii** require you to wave a controller but a camera on a computer can follow your movements using **touchless technology**. **AI** in computers could be able to monitor our mood and our health and work out what we need before we even know it!

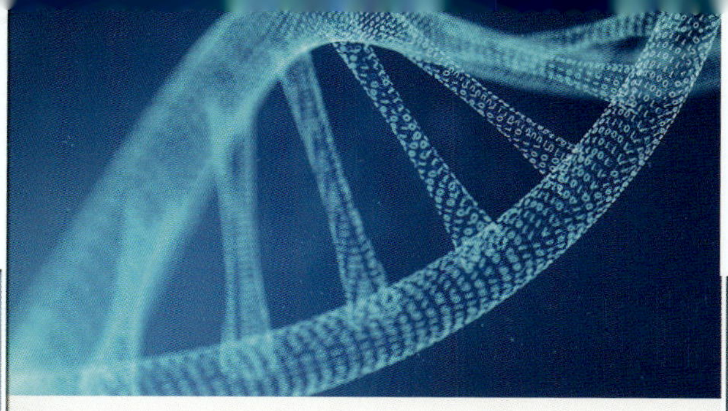

DNA DATA

Our bodies are biological machines, storing information on our genetic makeup in strings of DNA. Imagine if you could store computer data in DNA. This is what scientists are hoping to do with **DNA computers**. DNA molecules (what our genes are made of) can be used to perform complex mathematical problems many times faster than the world's most powerful human-built computers.

QUANTUM REALM

Most computers still use binary code as the basis of their calculations. Quantum computing goes a huge step further than these 1s and 0s by having the choice of 1, 0, and 1 or 0. These three states are called quantum bits or **qubits**. Results can be hard to read due to the strange nature of quantum mechanics. Quantum computers promise to be faster than any computer built so far, but they are only in development now.

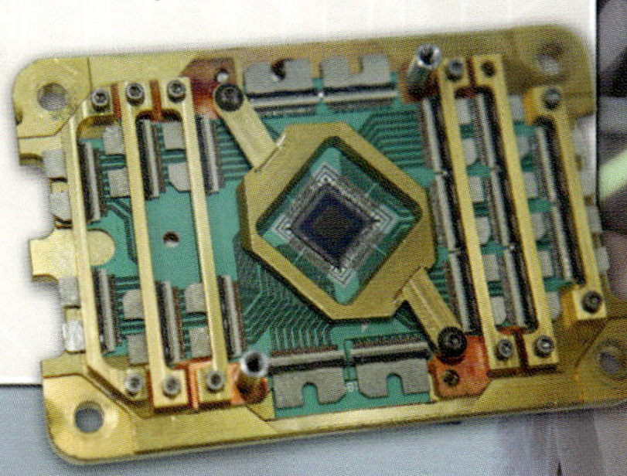

THINK AHEAD

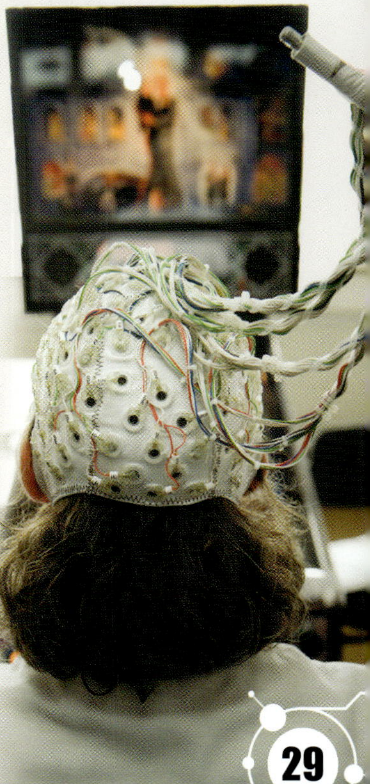

Soon you may not need to touch or speak to a computer to give it commands. Just think! **Brain-computer interfaces (BCI)** (right) are being developed to help people who are paralyzed or have severe motor disabilities communicate. Neurons in the brain pass on information through chemical and electrical signals. A BCI would receive the electrical signals as commands. We could be using computers as an extension of our bodies in the future. Are you ready for your upgrade?

GLOSSARY

Airbrush Physical or digital tool for adding soft layers of color to an image

Algorithm A set of rules or steps used in a calculation

App (Application) A software program

Artificial Intelligence (AI) Intelligence demonstrated by computers

Augmented Reality (AR) A real-world view with added computer-generated elements

Binary Number system based on 2 (0 and 1) rather than 10

Bit Binary unit (0 or 1)

Blogger Person who writes a website blog

Bluetooth Short-range wireless connection for smartphones and other devices

Brain-computer interface (BCI) Direct communication between a wired brain and a computer

Broadband Fast internet data transmission provided by a wide range of frequencies

Browser Program used to view web pages

Bug A code error in software

Byte Eight bits

Central processing unit (CPU) Microprocessor, the controlling hub of a computer

CEO (chief executive officer) The person with the most important position in a company

Cloud computing Use of servers, storage, and software over the internet

Computer-generated imagery (CGI) Special visual effects created on a computer

Cryptocurrency Digital money that does not exist as physical cash

Cyberattack Attempt by hackers to damage a computer system

Dark web Restricted part of the internet only seen through special software

Data Information used in a computer

Deep web Websites not found through search engines

DNA computing Computing using biochemistry instead of silicon chips

Emoji Digital icon used to express mood

Encryption Process of converting data into code that can only be unlocked by the receiver

Floppy disk A small soft piece of plastic that is protected by a hard cover and is used to store computer information

Global positioning system (GPS) A system that can show the exact position of a person or thing by using signals from satellites

Hacker A person who uses a computer to break into other computer networks

Hard drive Computer data storage device

Holographic Produced using light-beam-generated 3D images

Integrated circuit Electronic circuit set into a single piece of semi-conducting material, such as silicon

Joystick Lever used to control movement in a video game

Malware Malicious software used to illegally access or damage a computer

Microprocessor See central processing unit

Motherboard Main computer circuit holding CPU, memory, and hard-drive connections

Motion capture Process of recording an actor's movements and then using them to animate a digital character

Operating system (OS) Software that makes it easier for users to manage computer files and hardware

Petaflop a measure of computer performance

Quantum computing Use of quantum physics to compute at an atomic scale

Qubit Quantum bit (0, 1, and 0 or 1)

Random-access memory (RAM) A computer's short-term memory

Ransomware Malware that locks computer files and demands money to unlock them

Render In computing, completing a 3D image with full tones and color

Scammer Someone who uses emails to persuade you to part with money

Silicon Non-metal, semi-conducting material used in computer circuits

Software A program that gives instructions to a computer and controls what it does

Spam Unwanted emails

Spyware Software that records your actions on a computer without you knowing

Stream To listen to or watch sound or video on a computer directly from the internet

Stylus A pen-like tool used with a tablet

Supercomputer Powerful computer

Trackpad Touch-sensitive area on a computer used to give instructions

Transistor Small electronic device that amplifies current and switches it on and off

Trojan Malware disguised as trusted software

Virtual reality (VR) A computer-generated 3D environment

Virus Code that causes computer software problems

Web browser Software used to find information on the World Wide Web

WiFi A system allowing computers and other tech to communicate or go online without wires

World Wide Web The system of connected documents on the internet, usually with pictures, video, and sound, that can be searched for information about a particular subject

Worm Self-copying malware

Zombie computer Computer being used remotely without its owner's knowledge

FOR MORE INFORMATION

WEBSITES

Computer History Museum
Timeline of computers:
www.computerhistory.org/timeline/computers/

Explain That Stuff
Quantum Computing: www.explainthatstuff.com/quantum-computing.html

IBM Summit
World's most-powerful computer:
www.ibm.com/thought-leadership/summit-supercomputer/

Imperial War Museum
How Alan Turing cracked the Enigma Code:
www.iwm.org.uk/history/how-alan-turing-cracked-the-enigma-code

National Museum of Computing
World's largest collection of functional historic computers at Bletchley Park, UK:
www.tnmoc.org

Pixar
Science behind the animation studio:
sciencebehindpixar.org/pipeline/rendering

Raspberry Pi
Coding community:
www.raspberrypi.org

World's first website:
info.cern.ch

BOOKS

Adventures in STEAM: Computers, Claudia Martin (Wayland, 2017)

A World of Computers and Coding, Clive Gifford (Wayland, 2019)

Help Your Kids with Computer Science (DK)

Kid Engineer: Working with Computers and Robotics, Sonya Newland, (Wayland, 2020)

INDEX